This book belongs to:

What to Expect With This Garden Planner

Planning a garden is hard, especially in the beginning. You have no idea what to grow or where to start.
Congratulations, you have just found the best garden planner around!
No more guesswork when planning your garden!

Our five-year garden planner has everything you need to plan, record, and enjoy all your gardening activities in one place. Whether you're an experienced gardener or someone who wants to grow some herbs on their windowsill, this journal will help keep track of all the fun things that happen each season while inspiring you through quotes from famous people throughout history about gardens and nature.

This garden planner is a great way to keep track of all your garden projects, plans, and records in one place. The pages are broken into four stages: planning, sowing & planting, maintenance, and harvesting. There is plenty of space for writing down notes on what you plant where and how successful your garden was that year.

Included are forms for keeping track of expenses, making lists of plants that grow well together as companions, drawing out your dream plot, and keeping track of costs, annual tasks, project deadlines, and harvest yields. The forms are easy to fill out and make it simple to keep track of chores, issues that arise, and harvests.

How to Use the Garden Planner

The garden planner is designed to be used for five years. You can start using it in any year, but the best time to start is the year you are planning your garden. We suggest you do all the early work in pencil since lots can change once planting season begins.

The first step is planning your garden by writing down your goals for this year's garden. In the planning stage of each year, there are four styles of grids that you can use when planning your dream plot. The purpose of the various grids is to help you map out your garden and decide what plants to grow where. Start with the dot grid to make a rough draft before using the other grids to finalize your ideas.

You will also find charts to plan out projects that will be completed during the growing season and sheets to record expenses.

Once you have planned your garden, it is time to plant. To make it easy to keep track of what you plant, use your finalized garden planting chart. Included in the planting section are pages you will want to use to record the seeds and transplants that you placed in your garden, as well as a task planner and watering schedule pages.

Now that your garden is in place and growing, it is time to take care of it! Use the planner to reference what needs to be done each month quickly; this will help keep your garden healthy and look its best.

Finally, once you have harvested all your delicious fruits and vegetables, use the harvest yield form to record how much you got. This will help you plan your garden for the next year and determine what plants are worth growing again! All of the information you gather in this book will be used to keep track of what was happening in the garden.

Use the space at the end of each year for notes on what worked well in previous years and what didn't work as well so that next year's garden can be even better than before!

How to use the four plotting grids

1. Create a companion gardening chart.

You can do this by researching which vegetables grow well together and which should be planted away from one another.

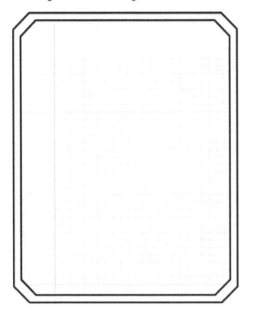

2. Use the dot grid to draw a rough draft of the garden plot.

Decide which direction your rows will run. Will you use wide rows or narrow rows? Remember to make walking paths.

3. Use the dot grid to create a color code chart to use on the row planners.

This is where you decide which plants will go into each row. Use your favorite coloring tools.

Ways you can customize your garden planner

Although the garden planner is laid out as a five-year garden planning book, it can be customized to fit any plan or garden schedule. You can start using it in any year and do not have to fill out every page if there are years you don't garden. This planner is a great organizational tool for gardeners of all levels.

As a bonus, we have included elements that you can color, so you can make your garden planner unique to your style.

There are no complex rules on using any of the pages since each garden is as unique as the gardener. This garden planner will help you stay organized throughout the season by noting everything in one place with helpful forms to fill out along the way.

We hope you'll find this planner to be a useful resource as you plan your best garden yet.

Happy gardening!

YEAR ONE

_____

Annual Planner

January	February	March
April	May	June
July	August	September
October	November	December

Goals

_____ ☐

_____ ☐

_____ ☐

_____ ☐

_____ ☐

EXPENSES

DATE	EXPENSE TYPE	CATEGORY	METHOD	AMOUNT
			TOTAL:	

EXPENSES

DATE	EXPENSE TYPE	CATEGORY	METHOD	AMOUNT
			TOTAL:	

Stage One: Planning

"It's spring fever. That is what the name of it is. And when you've got it, you want – oh, you don't quite know what it is you DO want, but it just fairly makes your heart ache, you want it so!"

– Huck Finn in Mark Twain's *Tom Sawyer, Detective,* 1896

Project to complete

project	
deadline	completed ☐

items required

tasks to-do

project	
deadline	completed ☐

items required

tasks to-do

Project to complete

project	
deadline	completed ☐

items required

tasks to-do

project	
deadline	completed ☐

items required

tasks to-do

Project to complete

project	
deadline	completed ☐

items required

tasks to-do

☐ _____
☐ _____
☐ _____
☐ _____
☐ _____
☐ _____

☐ _____
☐ _____
☐ _____
☐ _____
☐ _____
☐ _____

_____
_____
_____
_____
_____

project	
deadline	completed ☐

items required

tasks to-do

☐ _____
☐ _____
☐ _____
☐ _____
☐ _____
☐ _____

☐ _____
☐ _____
☐ _____
☐ _____
☐ _____
☐ _____

_____
_____
_____
_____
_____

Project to complete

project	
deadline	completed ☐

items required

tasks to-do

☐
☐
☐
☐
☐
☐

project	
deadline	completed ☐

items required

tasks to-do

☐
☐
☐
☐
☐
☐

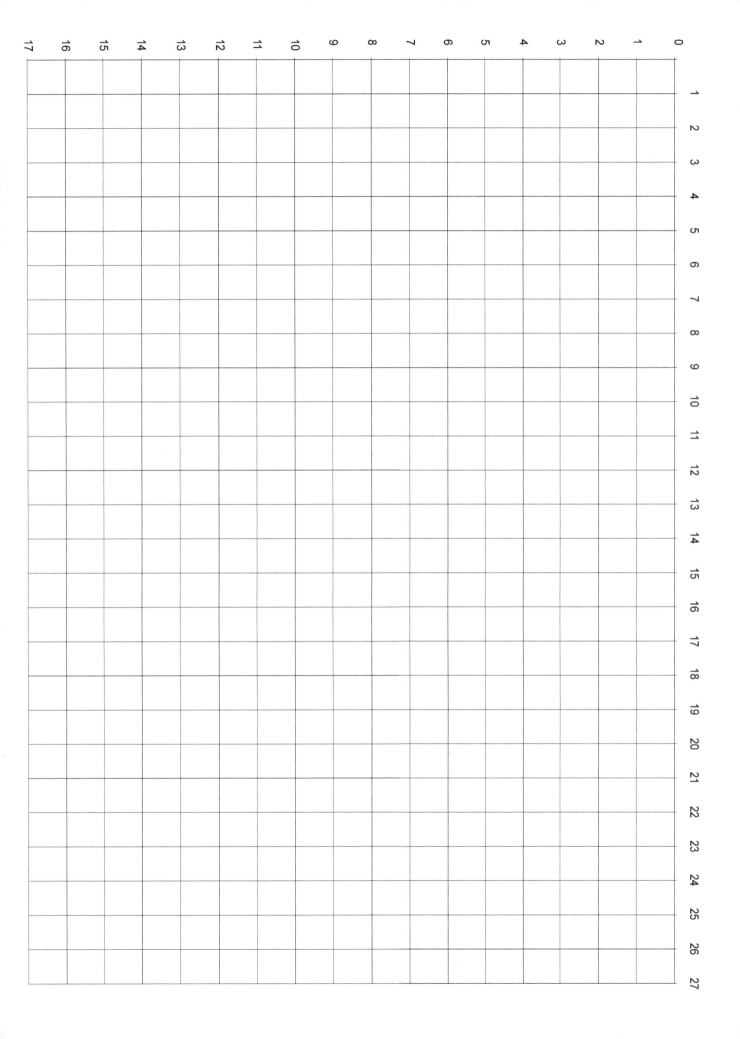

Stage Two: Sowing & Planting

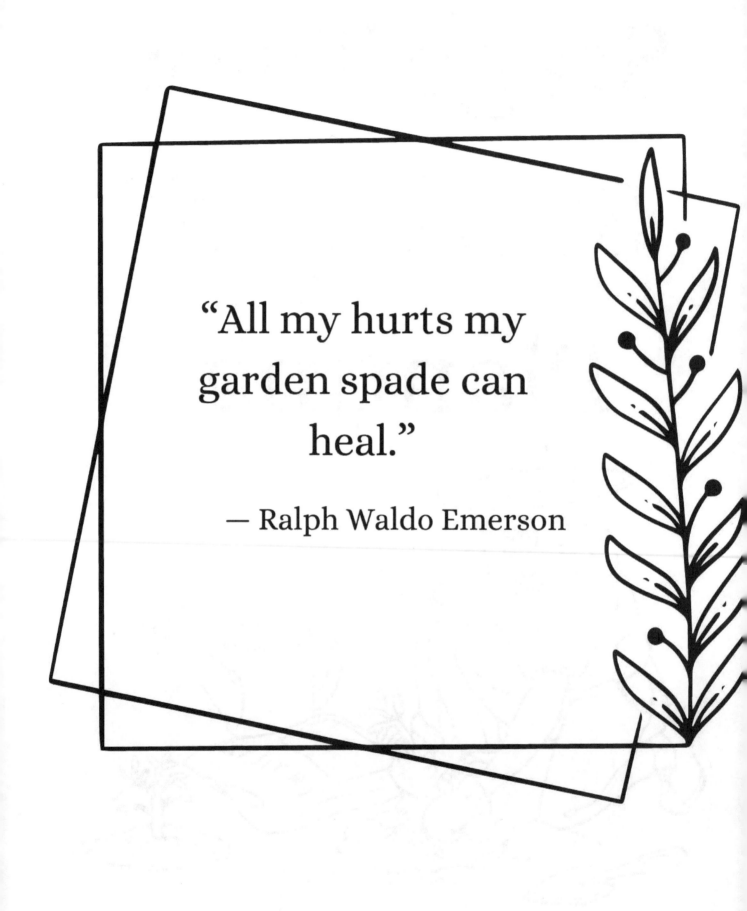

"All my hurts my garden spade can heal."

— Ralph Waldo Emerson

TASK	M	T	W	T	F	S	S
	☐	☐	☐	☐	☐	☐	☐
	☐	☐	☐	☐	☐	☐	☐
	☐	☐	☐	☐	☐	☐	☐
	☐	☐	☐	☐	☐	☐	☐
	☐	☐	☐	☐	☐	☐	☐
	☐	☐	☐	☐	☐	☐	☐
	☐	☐	☐	☐	☐	☐	☐
	☐	☐	☐	☐	☐	☐	☐
	☐	☐	☐	☐	☐	☐	☐
	☐	☐	☐	☐	☐	☐	☐
	☐	☐	☐	☐	☐	☐	☐
	☐	☐	☐	☐	☐	☐	☐
	☐	☐	☐	☐	☐	☐	☐
	☐	☐	☐	☐	☐	☐	☐
	☐	☐	☐	☐	☐	☐	☐
	☐	☐	☐	☐	☐	☐	☐

Seeds	Date Planted

Transplant	Date Planted

Seeds	Date Planted

Transplant	Date Planted

Monday

- ☐ _____
- ☐ _____
- ☐ _____
- ☐ _____

Tuesday

- ☐ _____
- ☐ _____
- ☐ _____
- ☐ _____

Wednesday

- ☐ _____
- ☐ _____
- ☐ _____
- ☐ _____

Thursday

- ☐ _____
- ☐ _____
- ☐ _____
- ☐ _____

Friday

- ☐ _____
- ☐ _____
- ☐ _____
- ☐ _____

Saturday

- ☐ _____
- ☐ _____
- ☐ _____
- ☐ _____

Sunday

- ☐ _____
- ☐ _____
- ☐ _____
- ☐ _____

Notes: _____
_____
_____
_____

Monday

_____

_____

_____

_____

Tuesday

- ☐ _____
- ☐ _____
- ☐ _____
- ☐ _____

Wednesday

_____

_____

_____

_____

Thursday

- ☐ _____
- ☐ _____
- ☐ _____
- ☐ _____

Friday

_____

_____

_____

_____

Saturday

- ☐ _____
- ☐ _____
- ☐ _____
- ☐ _____

Sunday

- ☐ _____
- ☐ _____
- ☐ _____
- ☐ _____

Notes: _____

_____

_____

_____

Monday

- ☐ _____
- ☐ _____
- ☐ _____
- ☐ _____

Tuesday

- ☐ _____
- ☐ _____
- ☐ _____
- ☐ _____

Wednesday

- ☐ _____
- ☐ _____
- ☐ _____
- ☐ _____

Thursday

- ☐ _____
- ☐ _____
- ☐ _____
- ☐ _____

Friday

- ☐ _____
- ☐ _____
- ☐ _____
- ☐ _____

Saturday

- ☐ _____
- ☐ _____
- ☐ _____
- ☐ _____

Sunday

- ☐ _____
- ☐ _____
- ☐ _____
- ☐ _____

Notes: _____
_____
_____
_____

Monday

_____

_____

_____

_____

Tuesday

☐ _____

☐ _____

☐ _____

☐ _____

Wednesday

_____

_____

_____

_____

Thursday

☐ _____

☐ _____

☐ _____

☐ _____

Friday

_____

_____

_____

_____

Saturday

☐ _____

☐ _____

☐ _____

☐ _____

Sunday

☐ _____

☐ _____

☐ _____

☐ _____

Notes: _____

_____

_____

_____

Stage Three: Maintenance

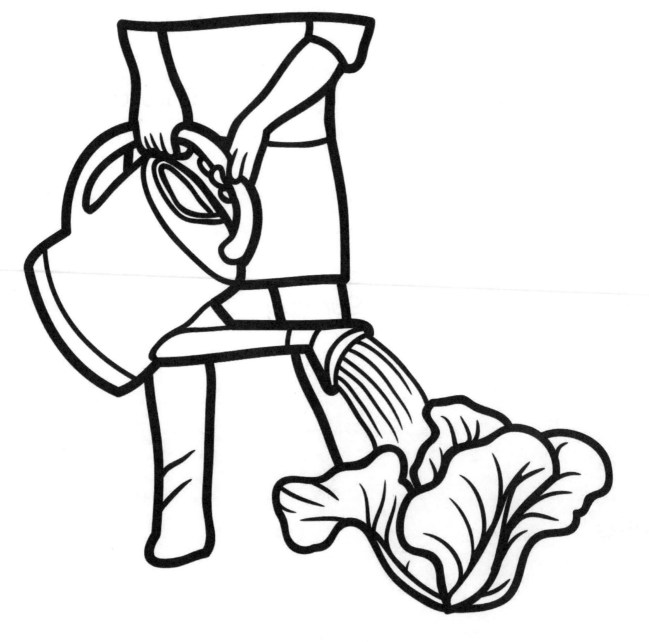

"The lesson I have thoroughly learned, and wish to pass on to others, is to know the enduring happiness that the love of a garden gives."

– Gertrude Jekyll, 1843-1932

TASK	M	T	W	T	F	S	S
	☐	☐	☐	☐	☐	☐	☐
	☐	☐	☐	☐	☐	☐	☐
	☐	☐	☐	☐	☐	☐	☐
	☐	☐	☐	☐	☐	☐	☐
	☐	☐	☐	☐	☐	☐	☐
	☐	☐	☐	☐	☐	☐	☐
	☐	☐	☐	☐	☐	☐	☐
	☐	☐	☐	☐	☐	☐	☐
	☐	☐	☐	☐	☐	☐	☐
	☐	☐	☐	☐	☐	☐	☐
	☐	☐	☐	☐	☐	☐	☐
	☐	☐	☐	☐	☐	☐	☐
	☐	☐	☐	☐	☐	☐	☐
	☐	☐	☐	☐	☐	☐	☐
	☐	☐	☐	☐	☐	☐	☐
	☐	☐	☐	☐	☐	☐	☐

TASK

	M	T	W	T	F	S	S
	☐	☐	☐	☐	☐	☐	☐
	☐	☐	☐	☐	☐	☐	☐
	☐	☐	☐	☐	☐	☐	☐
	☐	☐	☐	☐	☐	☐	☐
	☐	☐	☐	☐	☐	☐	☐
	☐	☐	☐	☐	☐	☐	☐
	☐	☐	☐	☐	☐	☐	☐
	☐	☐	☐	☐	☐	☐	☐
	☐	☐	☐	☐	☐	☐	☐
	☐	☐	☐	☐	☐	☐	☐
	☐	☐	☐	☐	☐	☐	☐
	☐	☐	☐	☐	☐	☐	☐
	☐	☐	☐	☐	☐	☐	☐
	☐	☐	☐	☐	☐	☐	☐
	☐	☐	☐	☐	☐	☐	☐
	☐	☐	☐	☐	☐	☐	☐

TASK	M	T	W	T	F	S	S
	☐	☐	☐	☐	☐	☐	☐
	☐	☐	☐	☐	☐	☐	☐
	☐	☐	☐	☐	☐	☐	☐
	☐	☐	☐	☐	☐	☐	☐
	☐	☐	☐	☐	☐	☐	☐
	☐	☐	☐	☐	☐	☐	☐
	☐	☐	☐	☐	☐	☐	☐
	☐	☐	☐	☐	☐	☐	☐
	☐	☐	☐	☐	☐	☐	☐
	☐	☐	☐	☐	☐	☐	☐
	☐	☐	☐	☐	☐	☐	☐
	☐	☐	☐	☐	☐	☐	☐
	☐	☐	☐	☐	☐	☐	☐
	☐	☐	☐	☐	☐	☐	☐
	☐	☐	☐	☐	☐	☐	☐
	☐	☐	☐	☐	☐	☐	☐

TASK	M	T	W	T	F	S	S
	☐	☐	☐	☐	☐	☐	☐
	☐	☐	☐	☐	☐	☐	☐
	☐	☐	☐	☐	☐	☐	☐
	☐	☐	☐	☐	☐	☐	☐
	☐	☐	☐	☐	☐	☐	☐
	☐	☐	☐	☐	☐	☐	☐
	☐	☐	☐	☐	☐	☐	☐
	☐	☐	☐	☐	☐	☐	☐
	☐	☐	☐	☐	☐	☐	☐
	☐	☐	☐	☐	☐	☐	☐
	☐	☐	☐	☐	☐	☐	☐
	☐	☐	☐	☐	☐	☐	☐
	☐	☐	☐	☐	☐	☐	☐
	☐	☐	☐	☐	☐	☐	☐
	☐	☐	☐	☐	☐	☐	☐
	☐	☐	☐	☐	☐	☐	☐

Stage Four: Harvest

"Gardening takes a plot of land, a hoe, and willing muscles. Scratching the soil, harvesting garden fruits, are peaceful results. With a garden, there is hope."

– Grace Firth, 1923-2004,

TASK	M	T	W	T	F	S	S
	☐	☐	☐	☐	☐	☐	☐
	☐	☐	☐	☐	☐	☐	☐
	☐	☐	☐	☐	☐	☐	☐
	☐	☐	☐	☐	☐	☐	☐
	☐	☐	☐	☐	☐	☐	☐
	☐	☐	☐	☐	☐	☐	☐
	☐	☐	☐	☐	☐	☐	☐
	☐	☐	☐	☐	☐	☐	☐
	☐	☐	☐	☐	☐	☐	☐
	☐	☐	☐	☐	☐	☐	☐
	☐	☐	☐	☐	☐	☐	☐
	☐	☐	☐	☐	☐	☐	☐
	☐	☐	☐	☐	☐	☐	☐
	☐	☐	☐	☐	☐	☐	☐
	☐	☐	☐	☐	☐	☐	☐
	☐	☐	☐	☐	☐	☐	☐

TASK	M	T	W	T	F	S	S
	☐	☐	☐	☐	☐	☐	☐
	☐	☐	☐	☐	☐	☐	☐
	☐	☐	☐	☐	☐	☐	☐
	☐	☐	☐	☐	☐	☐	☐
	☐	☐	☐	☐	☐	☐	☐
	☐	☐	☐	☐	☐	☐	☐
	☐	☐	☐	☐	☐	☐	☐
	☐	☐	☐	☐	☐	☐	☐
	☐	☐	☐	☐	☐	☐	☐
	☐	☐	☐	☐	☐	☐	☐
	☐	☐	☐	☐	☐	☐	☐
	☐	☐	☐	☐	☐	☐	☐
	☐	☐	☐	☐	☐	☐	☐
	☐	☐	☐	☐	☐	☐	☐
	☐	☐	☐	☐	☐	☐	☐
	☐	☐	☐	☐	☐	☐	☐

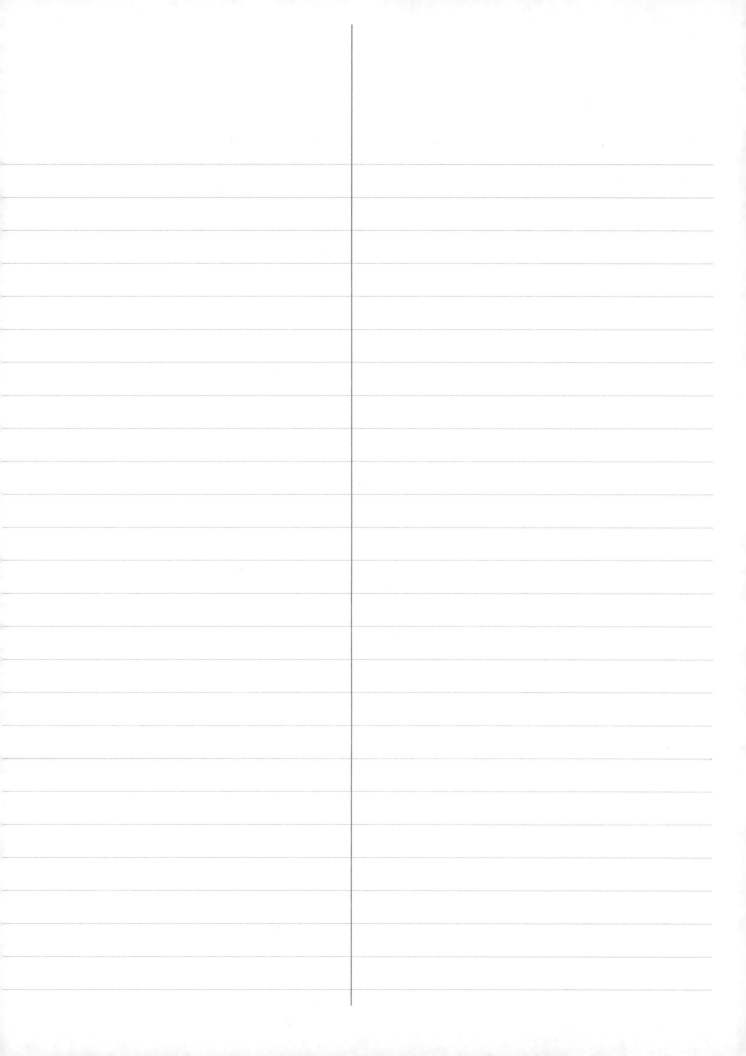

YEAR TWO

Annual Planner

January	February	March

April	May	June

July	August	September

October	November	December

Goals

EXPENSES

DATE	EXPENSE TYPE	CATEGORY	METHOD	AMOUNT
			TOTAL:	

EXPENSES

DATE	EXPENSE TYPE	CATEGORY	METHOD	AMOUNT
			TOTAL:	

Stage One: Planning

"I read [garden catalogs] for news, for driblets of knowledge, for aesthetic pleasure, and at the same time I am planning the future, so I read in dream."

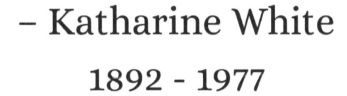

– Katharine White

1892 - 1977

Project to complete

project	
deadline	completed ☐

items required

tasks to-do

project	
deadline	completed ☐

items required

tasks to-do

Project to complete

project	
deadline	completed ☐

items required

tasks to-do

project	
deadline	completed ☐

items required

tasks to-do

Project to complete

project	
deadline	completed ☐

items required   tasks to-do

☐	
☐	
☐	
☐	
☐	
☐	

project	
deadline	completed ☐

items required   tasks to-do

☐	
☐	
☐	
☐	
☐	
☐	

Project to complete

project	
deadline	completed ☐

items required

tasks to-do

---

project	
deadline	completed ☐

items required

tasks to-do

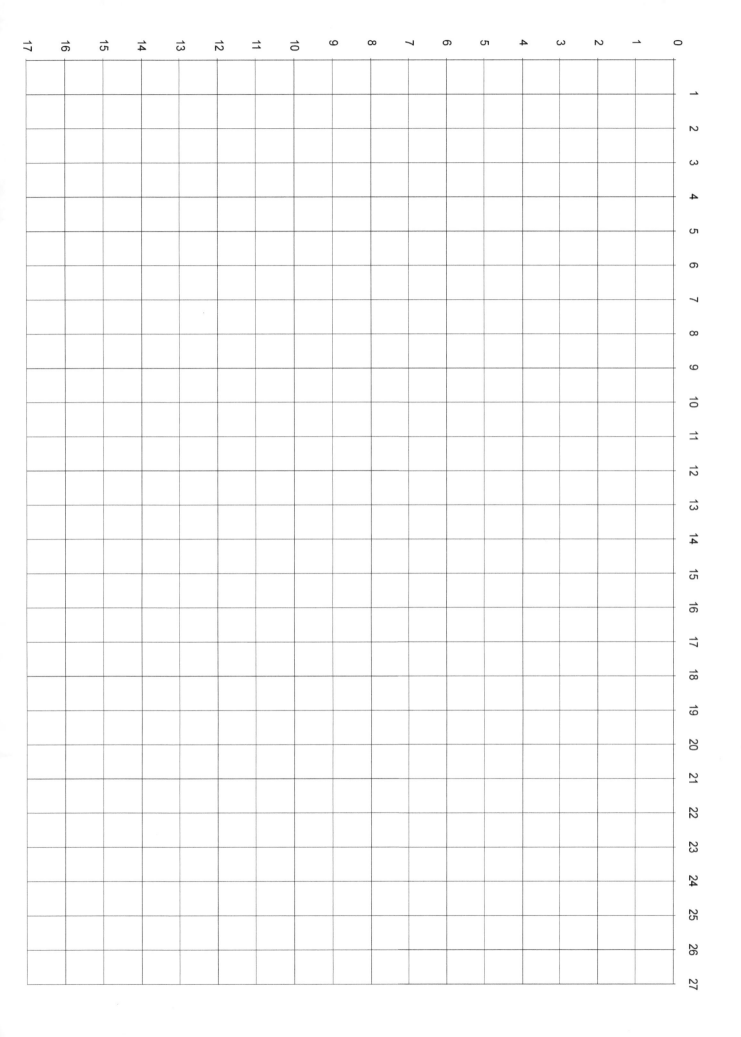

Stage Two: Sowing & Planting

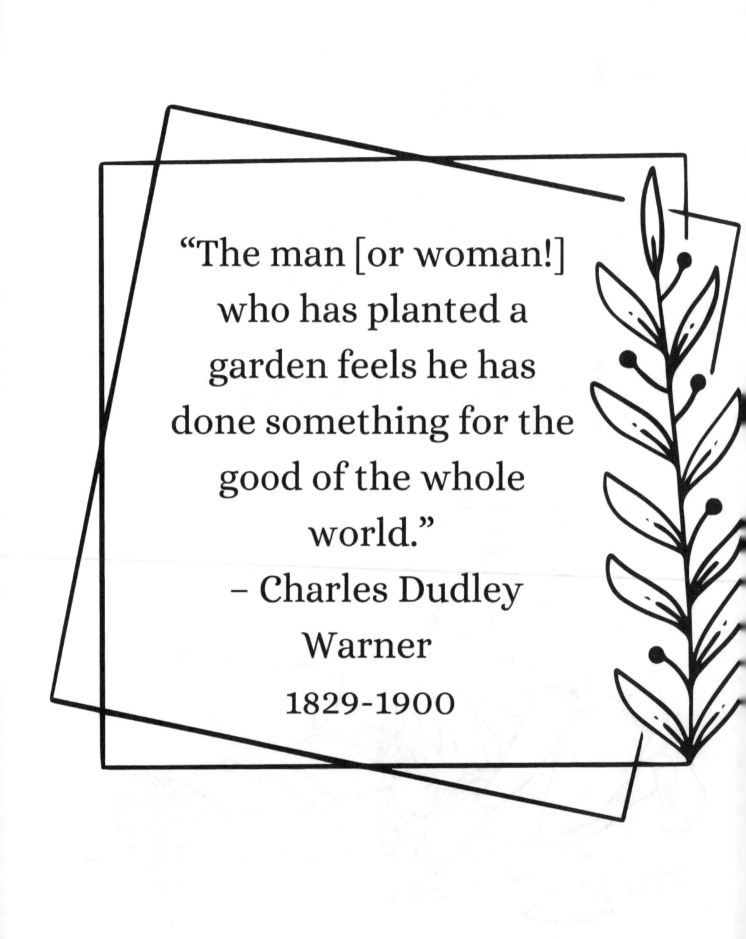

"The man [or woman!] who has planted a garden feels he has done something for the good of the whole world."

– Charles Dudley Warner

1829-1900

TASK	M	T	W	T	F	S	S
	☐	☐	☐	☐	☐	☐	☐
	☐	☐	☐	☐	☐	☐	☐
	☐	☐	☐	☐	☐	☐	☐
	☐	☐	☐	☐	☐	☐	☐
	☐	☐	☐	☐	☐	☐	☐
	☐	☐	☐	☐	☐	☐	☐
	☐	☐	☐	☐	☐	☐	☐
	☐	☐	☐	☐	☐	☐	☐
	☐	☐	☐	☐	☐	☐	☐
	☐	☐	☐	☐	☐	☐	☐
	☐	☐	☐	☐	☐	☐	☐
	☐	☐	☐	☐	☐	☐	☐
	☐	☐	☐	☐	☐	☐	☐
	☐	☐	☐	☐	☐	☐	☐
	☐	☐	☐	☐	☐	☐	☐
	☐	☐	☐	☐	☐	☐	☐

Seeds	Date Planted

Transplant	Date Planted

Seeds	Date Planted

Transplant	Date Planted

Monday

- [ ] _____
- [ ] _____
- [ ] _____
- [ ] _____

Tuesday

- [ ] _____
- [ ] _____
- [ ] _____
- [ ] _____

Wednesday

- [ ] _____
- [ ] _____
- [ ] _____
- [ ] _____

Thursday

- [ ] _____
- [ ] _____
- [ ] _____
- [ ] _____

Friday

- [ ] _____
- [ ] _____
- [ ] _____
- [ ] _____

Saturday

- [ ] _____
- [ ] _____
- [ ] _____
- [ ] _____

Sunday

- [ ] _____
- [ ] _____
- [ ] _____
- [ ] _____

Notes: _____

_____

_____

_____

Monday

_____

_____

_____

_____

Tuesday

- [ ] _____
- [ ] _____
- [ ] _____
- [ ] _____

Wednesday

_____

_____

_____

_____

Thursday

- [ ] _____
- [ ] _____
- [ ] _____
- [ ] _____

Friday

_____

_____

_____

_____

Saturday

- [ ] _____
- [ ] _____
- [ ] _____
- [ ] _____

Sunday

- [ ] _____
- [ ] _____
- [ ] _____
- [ ] _____

Notes: _____

_____

_____

_____

Monday

- [ ] _____
- [ ] _____
- [ ] _____
- [ ] _____

Tuesday

- [ ] _____
- [ ] _____
- [ ] _____
- [ ] _____

Wednesday

- [ ] _____
- [ ] _____
- [ ] _____
- [ ] _____

Thursday

- [ ] _____
- [ ] _____
- [ ] _____
- [ ] _____

Friday

- [ ] _____
- [ ] _____
- [ ] _____
- [ ] _____

Saturday

- [ ] _____
- [ ] _____
- [ ] _____
- [ ] _____

Sunday

- [ ] _____
- [ ] _____
- [ ] _____
- [ ] _____

Notes: _____

_____

_____

_____

Monday

_____

_____

_____

Tuesday

- ☐ _____
- ☐ _____
- ☐ _____
- ☐ _____

Wednesday

_____

_____

_____

Thursday

- ☐ _____
- ☐ _____
- ☐ _____
- ☐ _____

Friday

_____

_____

_____

Saturday

- ☐ _____
- ☐ _____
- ☐ _____
- ☐ _____

Sunday

- ☐ _____
- ☐ _____
- ☐ _____
- ☐ _____

Notes: _____

_____

_____

_____

Stage Three: Maintenance

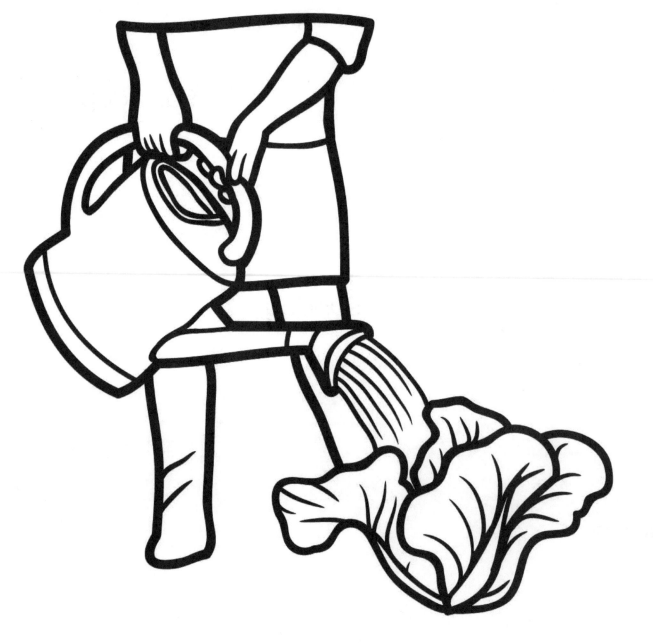

"Nature does not hurry, yet everything is accomplished"
– Lao Tzu

TASK	M	T	W	T	F	S	S
	☐	☐	☐	☐	☐	☐	☐
	☐	☐	☐	☐	☐	☐	☐
	☐	☐	☐	☐	☐	☐	☐
	☐	☐	☐	☐	☐	☐	☐
	☐	☐	☐	☐	☐	☐	☐
	☐	☐	☐	☐	☐	☐	☐
	☐	☐	☐	☐	☐	☐	☐
	☐	☐	☐	☐	☐	☐	☐
	☐	☐	☐	☐	☐	☐	☐
	☐	☐	☐	☐	☐	☐	☐
	☐	☐	☐	☐	☐	☐	☐
	☐	☐	☐	☐	☐	☐	☐
	☐	☐	☐	☐	☐	☐	☐
	☐	☐	☐	☐	☐	☐	☐
	☐	☐	☐	☐	☐	☐	☐
	☐	☐	☐	☐	☐	☐	☐

TASK

	M	T	W	T	F	S	S
	☐	☐	☐	☐	☐	☐	☐
	☐	☐	☐	☐	☐	☐	☐
	☐	☐	☐	☐	☐	☐	☐
	☐	☐	☐	☐	☐	☐	☐
	☐	☐	☐	☐	☐	☐	☐
	☐	☐	☐	☐	☐	☐	☐
	☐	☐	☐	☐	☐	☐	☐
	☐	☐	☐	☐	☐	☐	☐
	☐	☐	☐	☐	☐	☐	☐
	☐	☐	☐	☐	☐	☐	☐
	☐	☐	☐	☐	☐	☐	☐
	☐	☐	☐	☐	☐	☐	☐
	☐	☐	☐	☐	☐	☐	☐
	☐	☐	☐	☐	☐	☐	☐
	☐	☐	☐	☐	☐	☐	☐

TASK	M	T	W	T	F	S	S
	☐	☐	☐	☐	☐	☐	☐
	☐	☐	☐	☐	☐	☐	☐
	☐	☐	☐	☐	☐	☐	☐
	☐	☐	☐	☐	☐	☐	☐
	☐	☐	☐	☐	☐	☐	☐
	☐	☐	☐	☐	☐	☐	☐
	☐	☐	☐	☐	☐	☐	☐
	☐	☐	☐	☐	☐	☐	☐
	☐	☐	☐	☐	☐	☐	☐
	☐	☐	☐	☐	☐	☐	☐
	☐	☐	☐	☐	☐	☐	☐
	☐	☐	☐	☐	☐	☐	☐
	☐	☐	☐	☐	☐	☐	☐
	☐	☐	☐	☐	☐	☐	☐
	☐	☐	☐	☐	☐	☐	☐
	☐	☐	☐	☐	☐	☐	☐

TASK

	M	T	W	T	F	S	S
	☐	☐	☐	☐	☐	☐	☐
	☐	☐	☐	☐	☐	☐	☐
	☐	☐	☐	☐	☐	☐	☐
	☐	☐	☐	☐	☐	☐	☐
	☐	☐	☐	☐	☐	☐	☐
	☐	☐	☐	☐	☐	☐	☐
	☐	☐	☐	☐	☐	☐	☐
	☐	☐	☐	☐	☐	☐	☐
	☐	☐	☐	☐	☐	☐	☐
	☐	☐	☐	☐	☐	☐	☐
	☐	☐	☐	☐	☐	☐	☐
	☐	☐	☐	☐	☐	☐	☐
	☐	☐	☐	☐	☐	☐	☐
	☐	☐	☐	☐	☐	☐	☐
	☐	☐	☐	☐	☐	☐	☐
	☐	☐	☐	☐	☐	☐	☐

Stage Four: Harvest

"I believe a leaf of grass is no less than the journey-work of the stars . . .
And the running blackberry would adorn the parlors of heaven."

– Walt Whitman

1819-1892

TASK	M	T	W	T	F	S	S
	☐	☐	☐	☐	☐	☐	☐
	☐	☐	☐	☐	☐	☐	☐
	☐	☐	☐	☐	☐	☐	☐
	☐	☐	☐	☐	☐	☐	☐
	☐	☐	☐	☐	☐	☐	☐
	☐	☐	☐	☐	☐	☐	☐
	☐	☐	☐	☐	☐	☐	☐
	☐	☐	☐	☐	☐	☐	☐
	☐	☐	☐	☐	☐	☐	☐
	☐	☐	☐	☐	☐	☐	☐
	☐	☐	☐	☐	☐	☐	☐
	☐	☐	☐	☐	☐	☐	☐
	☐	☐	☐	☐	☐	☐	☐
	☐	☐	☐	☐	☐	☐	☐
	☐	☐	☐	☐	☐	☐	☐
	☐	☐	☐	☐	☐	☐	☐

TASK

	M	T	W	T	F	S	S
	☐	☐	☐	☐	☐	☐	☐
	☐	☐	☐	☐	☐	☐	☐
	☐	☐	☐	☐	☐	☐	☐
	☐	☐	☐	☐	☐	☐	☐
	☐	☐	☐	☐	☐	☐	☐
	☐	☐	☐	☐	☐	☐	☐
	☐	☐	☐	☐	☐	☐	☐
	☐	☐	☐	☐	☐	☐	☐
	☐	☐	☐	☐	☐	☐	☐
	☐	☐	☐	☐	☐	☐	☐
	☐	☐	☐	☐	☐	☐	☐
	☐	☐	☐	☐	☐	☐	☐
	☐	☐	☐	☐	☐	☐	☐
	☐	☐	☐	☐	☐	☐	☐
	☐	☐	☐	☐	☐	☐	☐
	☐	☐	☐	☐	☐	☐	☐

YEAR THREE

_____

Annual Planner

January	February	March
April	May	June
July	August	September
October	November	December

Goals

	☐
	☐
	☐
	☐
	☐

EXPENSES

DATE	EXPENSE TYPE	CATEGORY	METHOD	AMOUNT
			TOTAL:	

EXPENSES

DATE	EXPENSE TYPE	CATEGORY	METHOD	AMOUNT
			TOTAL:	

Stage One: Planning

"Aside from the garden of Eden, man's great temptation took place when he first received his seed catalog."
– Henry Wadsworth Longfellow
1807-1882

Project to complete

project	
deadline	completed ☐

items required

tasks to-do

☐ _____
☐ _____
☐ _____
☐ _____
☐ _____
☐ _____

☐ _____
☐ _____
☐ _____
☐ _____
☐ _____
☐ _____

project	
deadline	completed ☐

items required

tasks to-do

☐ _____
☐ _____
☐ _____
☐ _____
☐ _____
☐ _____

☐ _____
☐ _____
☐ _____
☐ _____
☐ _____
☐ _____

Project to complete

project	
deadline	completed ☐

items required

tasks to-do

---

project	
deadline	completed ☐

items required

tasks to-do

Project to complete

project	
deadline	completed ☐

items required

tasks to-do

project	
deadline	completed ☐

items required

tasks to-do

Project to complete

project	
deadline	completed ☐

items required

tasks to-do

☐

☐

☐

☐

☐

☐

project	
deadline	completed ☐

items required

tasks to-do

☐

☐

☐

☐

☐

☐

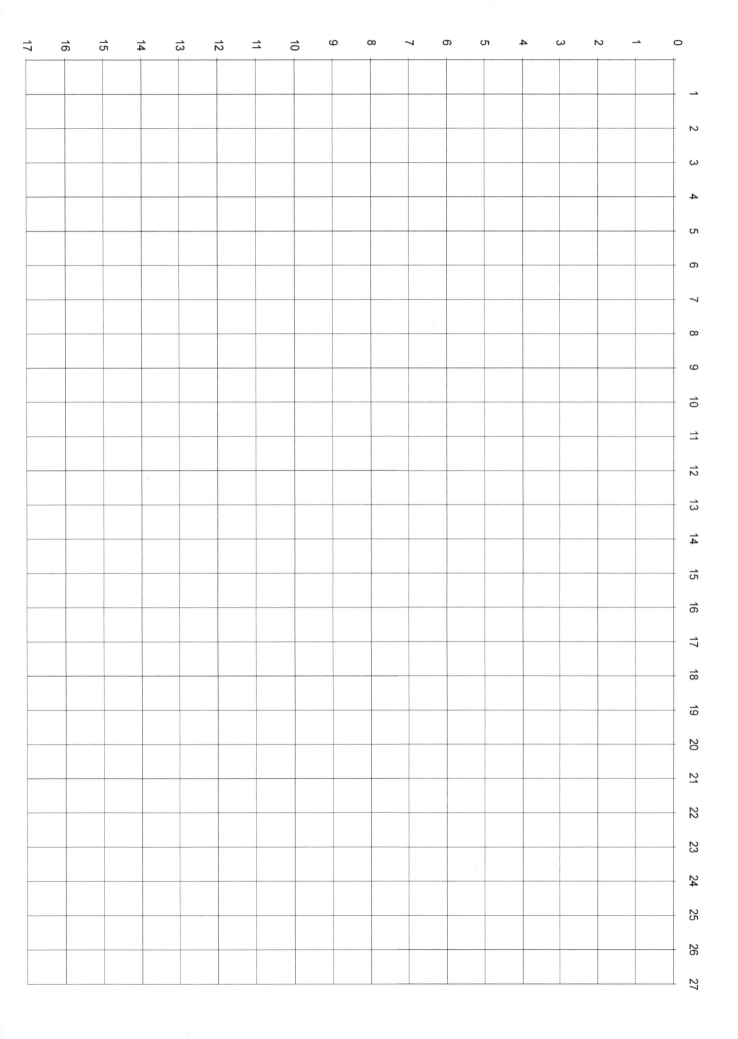

Stage Two: Sowing & Planting

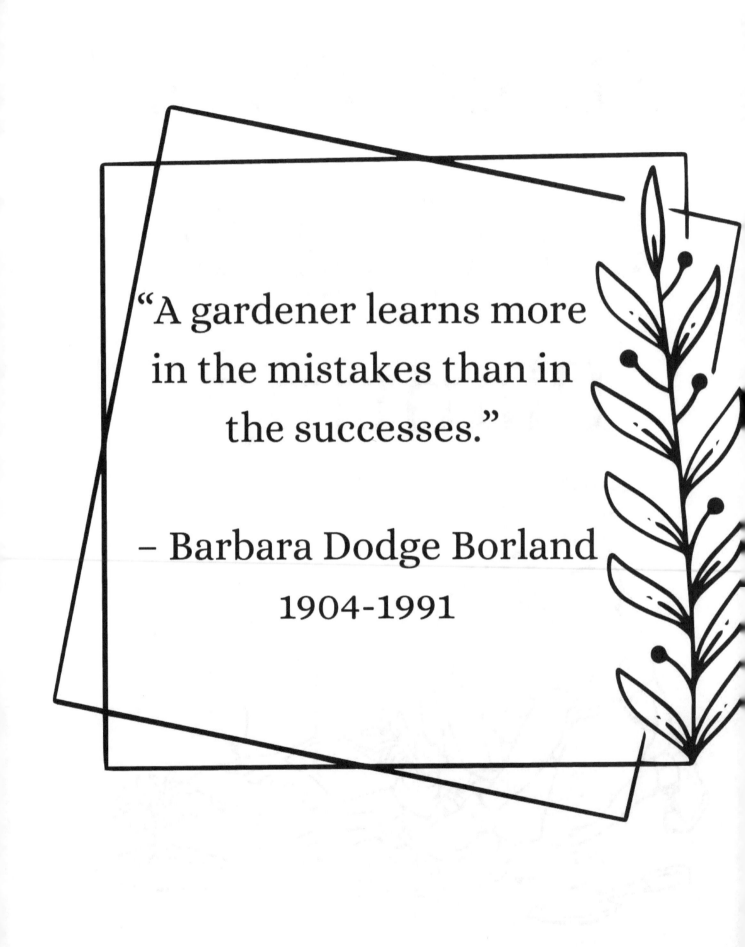

"A gardener learns more in the mistakes than in the successes."

– Barbara Dodge Borland
1904-1991

TASK	M	T	W	T	F	S	S
	☐	☐	☐	☐	☐	☐	☐
	☐	☐	☐	☐	☐	☐	☐
	☐	☐	☐	☐	☐	☐	☐
	☐	☐	☐	☐	☐	☐	☐
	☐	☐	☐	☐	☐	☐	☐
	☐	☐	☐	☐	☐	☐	☐
	☐	☐	☐	☐	☐	☐	☐
	☐	☐	☐	☐	☐	☐	☐
	☐	☐	☐	☐	☐	☐	☐
	☐	☐	☐	☐	☐	☐	☐
	☐	☐	☐	☐	☐	☐	☐
	☐	☐	☐	☐	☐	☐	☐
	☐	☐	☐	☐	☐	☐	☐
	☐	☐	☐	☐	☐	☐	☐
	☐	☐	☐	☐	☐	☐	☐
	☐	☐	☐	☐	☐	☐	☐

Seeds	Date Planted

Transplant	Date Planted

Seeds	Date Planted

Transplant	Date Planted

Monday

- [ ] _____
- [ ] _____
- [ ] _____
- [ ] _____

Tuesday

- [ ] _____
- [ ] _____
- [ ] _____
- [ ] _____

Wednesday

- [ ] _____
- [ ] _____
- [ ] _____
- [ ] _____

Thursday

- [ ] _____
- [ ] _____
- [ ] _____
- [ ] _____

Friday

- [ ] _____
- [ ] _____
- [ ] _____
- [ ] _____

Saturday

- [ ] _____
- [ ] _____
- [ ] _____
- [ ] _____

Sunday

- [ ] _____
- [ ] _____
- [ ] _____
- [ ] _____

Notes: _____
_____
_____
_____

Monday

_____

_____

_____

_____

Tuesday

☐ _____

☐ _____

☐ _____

☐ _____

Wednesday

_____

_____

_____

_____

Thursday

☐ _____

☐ _____

☐ _____

☐ _____

Friday

_____

_____

_____

_____

Saturday

☐ _____

☐ _____

☐ _____

☐ _____

Sunday

☐ _____

☐ _____

☐ _____

☐ _____

Notes: _____

_____

_____

_____

Monday

- ☐ _____
- ☐ _____
- ☐ _____
- ☐ _____

Tuesday

- ☐ _____
- ☐ _____
- ☐ _____
- ☐ _____

Wednesday

- ☐ _____
- ☐ _____
- ☐ _____
- ☐ _____

Thursday

- ☐ _____
- ☐ _____
- ☐ _____
- ☐ _____

Friday

- ☐ _____
- ☐ _____
- ☐ _____
- ☐ _____

Saturday

- ☐ _____
- ☐ _____
- ☐ _____
- ☐ _____

Sunday

- ☐ _____
- ☐ _____
- ☐ _____
- ☐ _____

Notes: _____

_____

_____

_____

Monday

_____

_____

_____

_____

Tuesday

- [ ] _____
- [ ] _____
- [ ] _____
- [ ] _____

Wednesday

_____

_____

_____

_____

Thursday

- [ ] _____
- [ ] _____
- [ ] _____
- [ ] _____

Friday

_____

_____

_____

_____

Saturday

- [ ] _____
- [ ] _____
- [ ] _____
- [ ] _____

Sunday

- [ ] _____
- [ ] _____
- [ ] _____
- [ ] _____

Notes: _____

_____

_____

_____

Stage Three: Maintenance

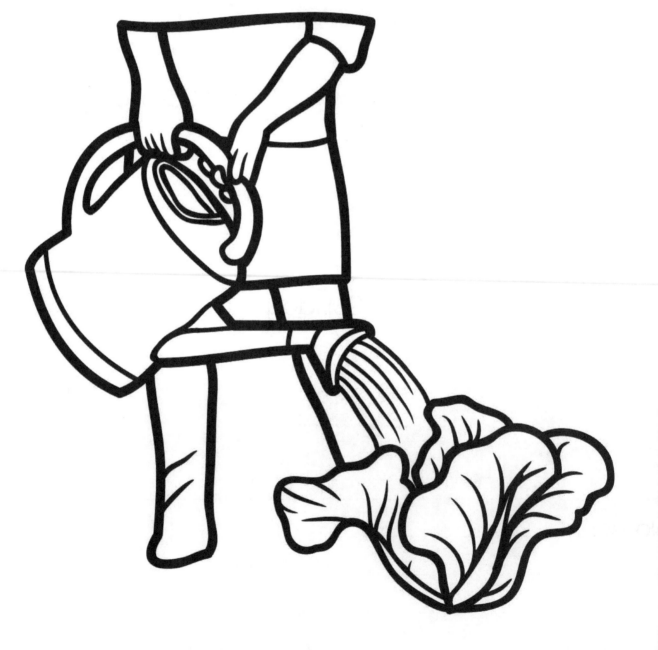

"The sun, with all those planets revolving around it and dependent on it, can still ripen a bunch of grapes as if it had nothing else in the universe to do."

– Galileo

1564-1642

TASK	M	T	W	T	F	S	S
	☐	☐	☐	☐	☐	☐	☐
	☐	☐	☐	☐	☐	☐	☐
	☐	☐	☐	☐	☐	☐	☐
	☐	☐	☐	☐	☐	☐	☐
	☐	☐	☐	☐	☐	☐	☐
	☐	☐	☐	☐	☐	☐	☐
	☐	☐	☐	☐	☐	☐	☐
	☐	☐	☐	☐	☐	☐	☐
	☐	☐	☐	☐	☐	☐	☐
	☐	☐	☐	☐	☐	☐	☐
	☐	☐	☐	☐	☐	☐	☐
	☐	☐	☐	☐	☐	☐	☐
	☐	☐	☐	☐	☐	☐	☐
	☐	☐	☐	☐	☐	☐	☐
	☐	☐	☐	☐	☐	☐	☐
	☐	☐	☐	☐	☐	☐	☐

TASK

	M	T	W	T	F	S	S
	☐	☐	☐	☐	☐	☐	☐
	☐	☐	☐	☐	☐	☐	☐
	☐	☐	☐	☐	☐	☐	☐
	☐	☐	☐	☐	☐	☐	☐
	☐	☐	☐	☐	☐	☐	☐
	☐	☐	☐	☐	☐	☐	☐
	☐	☐	☐	☐	☐	☐	☐
	☐	☐	☐	☐	☐	☐	☐
	☐	☐	☐	☐	☐	☐	☐
	☐	☐	☐	☐	☐	☐	☐
	☐	☐	☐	☐	☐	☐	☐
	☐	☐	☐	☐	☐	☐	☐
	☐	☐	☐	☐	☐	☐	☐
	☐	☐	☐	☐	☐	☐	☐
	☐	☐	☐	☐	☐	☐	☐
	☐	☐	☐	☐	☐	☐	☐

TASK	M	T	W	T	F	S	S
	☐	☐	☐	☐	☐	☐	☐
	☐	☐	☐	☐	☐	☐	☐
	☐	☐	☐	☐	☐	☐	☐
	☐	☐	☐	☐	☐	☐	☐
	☐	☐	☐	☐	☐	☐	☐
	☐	☐	☐	☐	☐	☐	☐
	☐	☐	☐	☐	☐	☐	☐
	☐	☐	☐	☐	☐	☐	☐
	☐	☐	☐	☐	☐	☐	☐
	☐	☐	☐	☐	☐	☐	☐
	☐	☐	☐	☐	☐	☐	☐
	☐	☐	☐	☐	☐	☐	☐
	☐	☐	☐	☐	☐	☐	☐
	☐	☐	☐	☐	☐	☐	☐
	☐	☐	☐	☐	☐	☐	☐
	☐	☐	☐	☐	☐	☐	☐

TASK	M	T	W	T	F	S	S
	☐	☐	☐	☐	☐	☐	☐
	☐	☐	☐	☐	☐	☐	☐
	☐	☐	☐	☐	☐	☐	☐
	☐	☐	☐	☐	☐	☐	☐
	☐	☐	☐	☐	☐	☐	☐
	☐	☐	☐	☐	☐	☐	☐
	☐	☐	☐	☐	☐	☐	☐
	☐	☐	☐	☐	☐	☐	☐
	☐	☐	☐	☐	☐	☐	☐
	☐	☐	☐	☐	☐	☐	☐
	☐	☐	☐	☐	☐	☐	☐
	☐	☐	☐	☐	☐	☐	☐
	☐	☐	☐	☐	☐	☐	☐
	☐	☐	☐	☐	☐	☐	☐
	☐	☐	☐	☐	☐	☐	☐
	☐	☐	☐	☐	☐	☐	☐

Stage Four: Harvest

"Good gardeners are always young in spirit, for their minds are fixed on spring when others feel only the bitter sting of winter."
– Mary Fanton-Roberts
1864-1956

TASK	M	T	W	T	F	S	S
	☐	☐	☐	☐	☐	☐	☐
	☐	☐	☐	☐	☐	☐	☐
	☐	☐	☐	☐	☐	☐	☐
	☐	☐	☐	☐	☐	☐	☐
	☐	☐	☐	☐	☐	☐	☐
	☐	☐	☐	☐	☐	☐	☐
	☐	☐	☐	☐	☐	☐	☐
	☐	☐	☐	☐	☐	☐	☐
	☐	☐	☐	☐	☐	☐	☐
	☐	☐	☐	☐	☐	☐	☐
	☐	☐	☐	☐	☐	☐	☐
	☐	☐	☐	☐	☐	☐	☐
	☐	☐	☐	☐	☐	☐	☐
	☐	☐	☐	☐	☐	☐	☐
	☐	☐	☐	☐	☐	☐	☐
	☐	☐	☐	☐	☐	☐	☐

TASK	M	T	W	T	F	S	S
	☐	☐	☐	☐	☐	☐	☐
	☐	☐	☐	☐	☐	☐	☐
	☐	☐	☐	☐	☐	☐	☐
	☐	☐	☐	☐	☐	☐	☐
	☐	☐	☐	☐	☐	☐	☐
	☐	☐	☐	☐	☐	☐	☐
	☐	☐	☐	☐	☐	☐	☐
	☐	☐	☐	☐	☐	☐	☐
	☐	☐	☐	☐	☐	☐	☐
	☐	☐	☐	☐	☐	☐	☐
	☐	☐	☐	☐	☐	☐	☐
	☐	☐	☐	☐	☐	☐	☐
	☐	☐	☐	☐	☐	☐	☐
	☐	☐	☐	☐	☐	☐	☐
	☐	☐	☐	☐	☐	☐	☐
	☐	☐	☐	☐	☐	☐	☐

YEAR FOUR

Annual Planner

January	February	March

April	May	June

July	August	September

October	November	December

Goals

EXPENSES

DATE	EXPENSE TYPE	CATEGORY	METHOD	AMOUNT
			TOTAL:	

XPENSES

DATE	EXPENSE TYPE	CATEGORY	METHOD	AMOUNT
			TOTAL:	

Stage One: Planning

"Everybody needs beauty as well as bread, places to play in and pray in, where nature may heal and give strength to body and soul alike."
– John Muir
1838-1914

Project to complete

project	
deadline	completed ☐

items required   tasks to-do

☐
☐
☐
☐
☐
☐

☐
☐
☐
☐
☐
☐

project	
deadline	completed ☐

items required   tasks to-do

☐
☐
☐
☐
☐
☐

☐
☐
☐
☐
☐
☐

Project to complete

project	
deadline	completed ☐

items required

tasks to-do

project	
deadline	completed ☐

items required

tasks to-do

Project to complete

project	
deadline	completed ☐

items required

tasks to-do

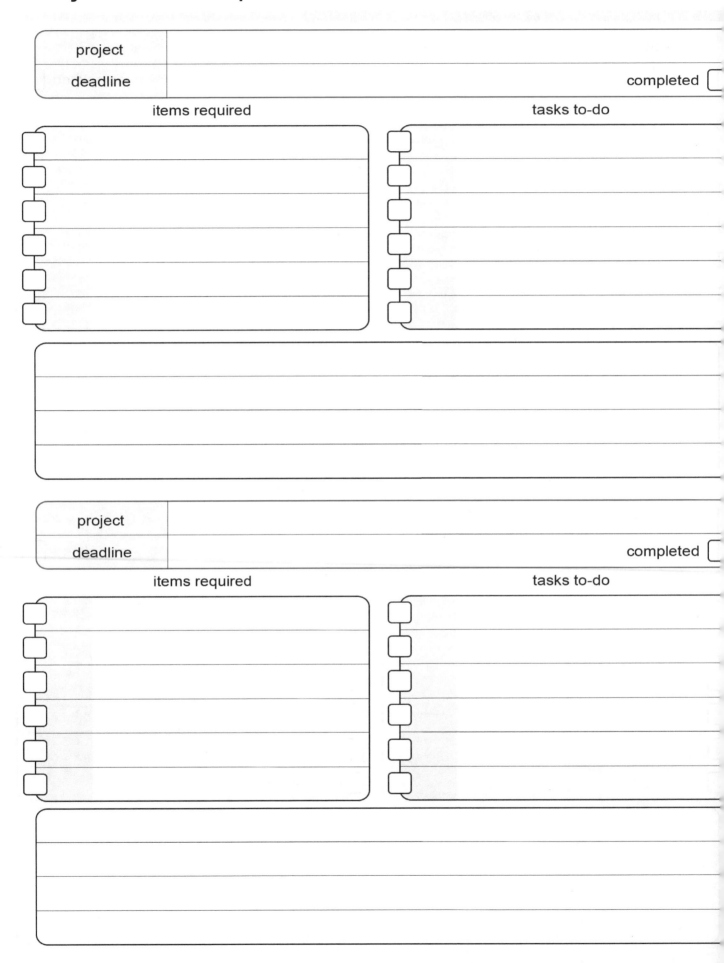

project	
deadline	completed ☐

items required

tasks to-do

Project to complete

project	
deadline	completed ☐

items required

tasks to-do

project	
deadline	completed ☐

items required

tasks to-do

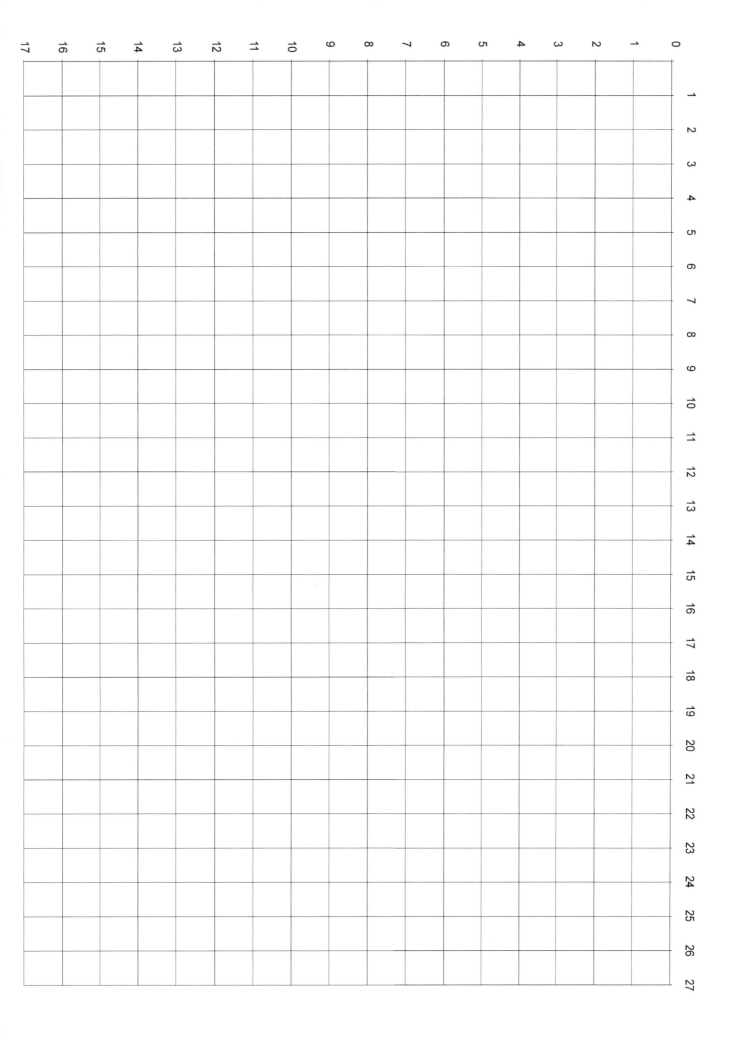

Stage Two: Sowing & Planting

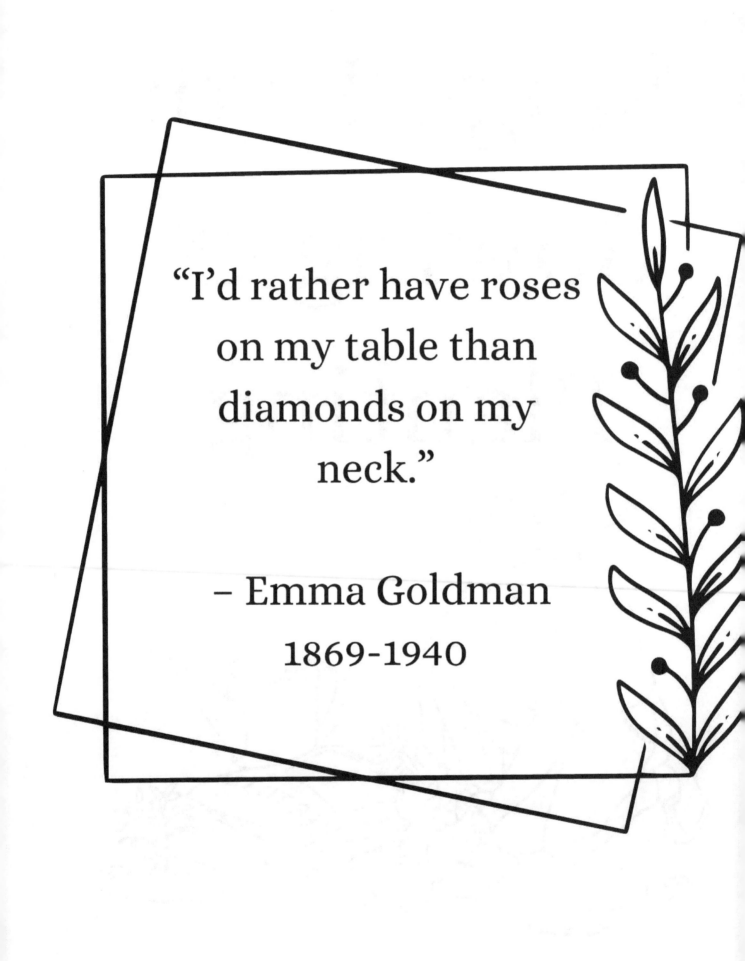

"I'd rather have roses on my table than diamonds on my neck."

– Emma Goldman
1869-1940

TASK	M	T	W	T	F	S	S
	☐	☐	☐	☐	☐	☐	☐
	☐	☐	☐	☐	☐	☐	☐
	☐	☐	☐	☐	☐	☐	☐
	☐	☐	☐	☐	☐	☐	☐
	☐	☐	☐	☐	☐	☐	☐
	☐	☐	☐	☐	☐	☐	☐
	☐	☐	☐	☐	☐	☐	☐
	☐	☐	☐	☐	☐	☐	☐
	☐	☐	☐	☐	☐	☐	☐
	☐	☐	☐	☐	☐	☐	☐
	☐	☐	☐	☐	☐	☐	☐
	☐	☐	☐	☐	☐	☐	☐
	☐	☐	☐	☐	☐	☐	☐
	☐	☐	☐	☐	☐	☐	☐
	☐	☐	☐	☐	☐	☐	☐
	☐	☐	☐	☐	☐	☐	☐

Seeds	Date Planted

Transplant	Date Planted

Seeds	Date Planted

Transplant	Date Planted

Monday

- [ ] _____
- [ ] _____
- [ ] _____
- [ ] _____

Tuesday

- [ ] _____
- [ ] _____
- [ ] _____
- [ ] _____

Wednesday

- [ ] _____
- [ ] _____
- [ ] _____
- [ ] _____

Thursday

- [ ] _____
- [ ] _____
- [ ] _____
- [ ] _____

Friday

- [ ] _____
- [ ] _____
- [ ] _____
- [ ] _____

Saturday

- [ ] _____
- [ ] _____
- [ ] _____
- [ ] _____

Sunday

- [ ] _____
- [ ] _____
- [ ] _____
- [ ] _____

Notes: _____
_____
_____
_____

Monday

_____
_____
_____
_____

Tuesday

- [ ] _____
- [ ] _____
- [ ] _____
- [ ] _____

Wednesday

_____
_____
_____
_____

Thursday

- [ ] _____
- [ ] _____
- [ ] _____
- [ ] _____

Friday

_____
_____
_____
_____

Saturday

- [ ] _____
- [ ] _____
- [ ] _____
- [ ] _____

Sunday

- [ ] _____
- [ ] _____
- [ ] _____
- [ ] _____

Notes: _____
_____
_____
_____

Monday

- [ ] _____
- [ ] _____
- [ ] _____
- [ ] _____

Tuesday

- [ ] _____
- [ ] _____
- [ ] _____
- [ ] _____

Wednesday

- [ ] _____
- [ ] _____
- [ ] _____
- [ ] _____

Thursday

- [ ] _____
- [ ] _____
- [ ] _____
- [ ] _____

Friday

- [ ] _____
- [ ] _____
- [ ] _____
- [ ] _____

Saturday

- [ ] _____
- [ ] _____
- [ ] _____
- [ ] _____

Sunday

- [ ] _____
- [ ] _____
- [ ] _____
- [ ] _____

Notes: _____

_____

_____

_____

Monday

_____

_____

_____

_____

Tuesday

- [ ] _____
- [ ] _____
- [ ] _____
- [ ] _____

Wednesday

_____

_____

_____

_____

Thursday

- [ ] _____
- [ ] _____
- [ ] _____
- [ ] _____

Friday

_____

_____

_____

_____

Saturday

- [ ] _____
- [ ] _____
- [ ] _____
- [ ] _____

Sunday

- [ ] _____
- [ ] _____
- [ ] _____
- [ ] _____

Notes: _____

_____

_____

_____

Stage Three: Maintenance

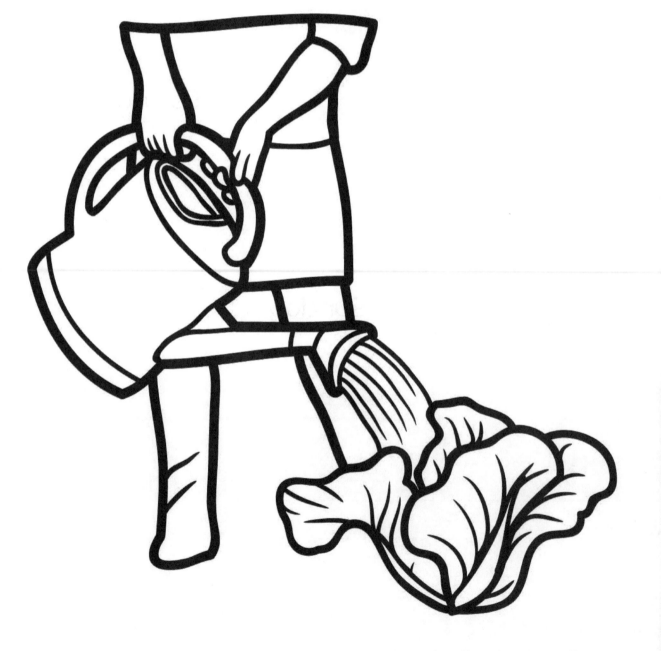

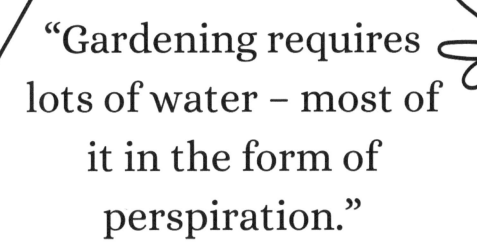

"Gardening requires lots of water – most of it in the form of perspiration."

– Lou Erickson

1913-1990

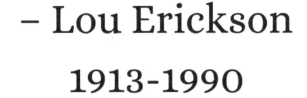

TASK	M	T	W	T	F	S	S
	☐	☐	☐	☐	☐	☐	☐
	☐	☐	☐	☐	☐	☐	☐
	☐	☐	☐	☐	☐	☐	☐
	☐	☐	☐	☐	☐	☐	☐
	☐	☐	☐	☐	☐	☐	☐
	☐	☐	☐	☐	☐	☐	☐
	☐	☐	☐	☐	☐	☐	☐
	☐	☐	☐	☐	☐	☐	☐
	☐	☐	☐	☐	☐	☐	☐
	☐	☐	☐	☐	☐	☐	☐
	☐	☐	☐	☐	☐	☐	☐
	☐	☐	☐	☐	☐	☐	☐
	☐	☐	☐	☐	☐	☐	☐
	☐	☐	☐	☐	☐	☐	☐
	☐	☐	☐	☐	☐	☐	☐
	☐	☐	☐	☐	☐	☐	☐

TASK	M	T	W	T	F	S	S
	☐	☐	☐	☐	☐	☐	☐
	☐	☐	☐	☐	☐	☐	☐
	☐	☐	☐	☐	☐	☐	☐
	☐	☐	☐	☐	☐	☐	☐
	☐	☐	☐	☐	☐	☐	☐
	☐	☐	☐	☐	☐	☐	☐
	☐	☐	☐	☐	☐	☐	☐
	☐	☐	☐	☐	☐	☐	☐
	☐	☐	☐	☐	☐	☐	☐
	☐	☐	☐	☐	☐	☐	☐
	☐	☐	☐	☐	☐	☐	☐
	☐	☐	☐	☐	☐	☐	☐
	☐	☐	☐	☐	☐	☐	☐
	☐	☐	☐	☐	☐	☐	☐
	☐	☐	☐	☐	☐	☐	☐
	☐	☐	☐	☐	☐	☐	☐

TASK	M	T	W	T	F	S	S
	☐	☐	☐	☐	☐	☐	☐
	☐	☐	☐	☐	☐	☐	☐
	☐	☐	☐	☐	☐	☐	☐
	☐	☐	☐	☐	☐	☐	☐
	☐	☐	☐	☐	☐	☐	☐
	☐	☐	☐	☐	☐	☐	☐
	☐	☐	☐	☐	☐	☐	☐
	☐	☐	☐	☐	☐	☐	☐
	☐	☐	☐	☐	☐	☐	☐
	☐	☐	☐	☐	☐	☐	☐
	☐	☐	☐	☐	☐	☐	☐
	☐	☐	☐	☐	☐	☐	☐
	☐	☐	☐	☐	☐	☐	☐
	☐	☐	☐	☐	☐	☐	☐
	☐	☐	☐	☐	☐	☐	☐
	☐	☐	☐	☐	☐	☐	☐

TASK	M	T	W	T	F	S	S
	☐	☐	☐	☐	☐	☐	☐
	☐	☐	☐	☐	☐	☐	☐
	☐	☐	☐	☐	☐	☐	☐
	☐	☐	☐	☐	☐	☐	☐
	☐	☐	☐	☐	☐	☐	☐
	☐	☐	☐	☐	☐	☐	☐
	☐	☐	☐	☐	☐	☐	☐
	☐	☐	☐	☐	☐	☐	☐
	☐	☐	☐	☐	☐	☐	☐
	☐	☐	☐	☐	☐	☐	☐
	☐	☐	☐	☐	☐	☐	☐
	☐	☐	☐	☐	☐	☐	☐
	☐	☐	☐	☐	☐	☐	☐
	☐	☐	☐	☐	☐	☐	☐
	☐	☐	☐	☐	☐	☐	☐
	☐	☐	☐	☐	☐	☐	☐

Stage Four: Harvest

"Don't judge each day by the harvest you reap, but by the seeds [and bulbs!] you plant."

– Robert Louis Stevenson

1850-1894

TASK	M	T	W	T	F	S	S
	☐	☐	☐	☐	☐	☐	☐
	☐	☐	☐	☐	☐	☐	☐
	☐	☐	☐	☐	☐	☐	☐
	☐	☐	☐	☐	☐	☐	☐
	☐	☐	☐	☐	☐	☐	☐
	☐	☐	☐	☐	☐	☐	☐
	☐	☐	☐	☐	☐	☐	☐
	☐	☐	☐	☐	☐	☐	☐
	☐	☐	☐	☐	☐	☐	☐
	☐	☐	☐	☐	☐	☐	☐
	☐	☐	☐	☐	☐	☐	☐
	☐	☐	☐	☐	☐	☐	☐
	☐	☐	☐	☐	☐	☐	☐
	☐	☐	☐	☐	☐	☐	☐
	☐	☐	☐	☐	☐	☐	☐
	☐	☐	☐	☐	☐	☐	☐

TASK	M	T	W	T	F	S	S
	☐	☐	☐	☐	☐	☐	☐
	☐	☐	☐	☐	☐	☐	☐
	☐	☐	☐	☐	☐	☐	☐
	☐	☐	☐	☐	☐	☐	☐
	☐	☐	☐	☐	☐	☐	☐
	☐	☐	☐	☐	☐	☐	☐
	☐	☐	☐	☐	☐	☐	☐
	☐	☐	☐	☐	☐	☐	☐
	☐	☐	☐	☐	☐	☐	☐
	☐	☐	☐	☐	☐	☐	☐
	☐	☐	☐	☐	☐	☐	☐
	☐	☐	☐	☐	☐	☐	☐
	☐	☐	☐	☐	☐	☐	☐
	☐	☐	☐	☐	☐	☐	☐
	☐	☐	☐	☐	☐	☐	☐

YEAR FIVE

Annual Planner

January	February	March
April	May	June
July	August	September
October	November	December

Goals

	☐
	☐
	☐
	☐
	☐

EXPENSES

DATE	EXPENSE TYPE	CATEGORY	METHOD	AMOUNT
			TOTAL:	

XPENSES

DATE	EXPENSE TYPE	CATEGORY	METHOD	AMOUNT
			TOTAL:	

Stage One: Planning

"If you have a garden and a library, you have everything you need."

– Cicero

106-43 BCE

Project to complete

project	
deadline	completed ☐

items required

☐ _____
☐ _____
☐ _____
☐ _____
☐ _____
☐ _____

tasks to-do

☐ _____
☐ _____
☐ _____
☐ _____
☐ _____
☐ _____

_____
_____
_____
_____

project	
deadline	completed ☐

items required

☐ _____
☐ _____
☐ _____
☐ _____
☐ _____
☐ _____

tasks to-do

☐ _____
☐ _____
☐ _____
☐ _____
☐ _____
☐ _____

_____
_____
_____
_____

Project to complete

project	
deadline	completed ☐

items required

tasks to-do

project	
deadline	completed ☐

items required

tasks to-do

Project to complete

project	
deadline	completed ☐

items required

- ☐
- ☐
- ☐
- ☐
- ☐
- ☐

tasks to-do

- ☐
- ☐
- ☐
- ☐
- ☐
- ☐

project	
deadline	completed ☐

items required

- ☐
- ☐
- ☐
- ☐
- ☐
- ☐

tasks to-do

- ☐
- ☐
- ☐
- ☐
- ☐
- ☐

Project to complete

project	
deadline	completed ☐

items required

tasks to-do

---

project	
deadline	completed ☐

items required

tasks to-do

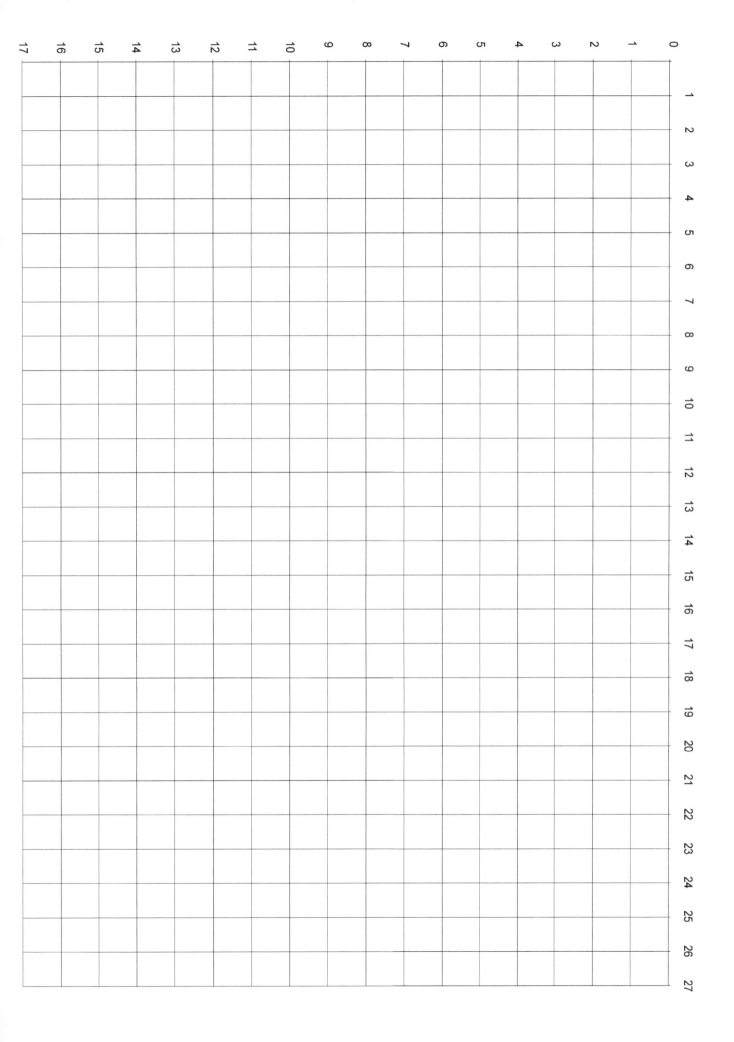

Stage Two: Sowing & Planting

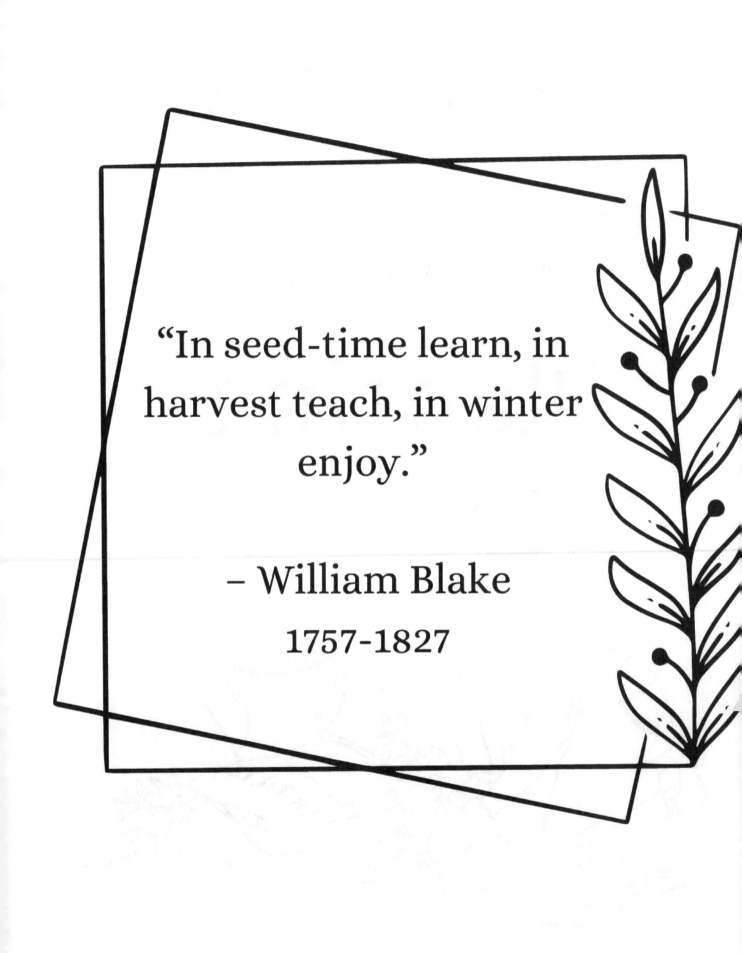

"In seed-time learn, in harvest teach, in winter enjoy."

– William Blake

1757-1827

TASK	M	T	W	T	F	S	S
	☐	☐	☐	☐	☐	☐	☐
	☐	☐	☐	☐	☐	☐	☐
	☐	☐	☐	☐	☐	☐	☐
	☐	☐	☐	☐	☐	☐	☐
	☐	☐	☐	☐	☐	☐	☐
	☐	☐	☐	☐	☐	☐	☐
	☐	☐	☐	☐	☐	☐	☐
	☐	☐	☐	☐	☐	☐	☐
	☐	☐	☐	☐	☐	☐	☐
	☐	☐	☐	☐	☐	☐	☐
	☐	☐	☐	☐	☐	☐	☐
	☐	☐	☐	☐	☐	☐	☐
	☐	☐	☐	☐	☐	☐	☐
	☐	☐	☐	☐	☐	☐	☐
	☐	☐	☐	☐	☐	☐	☐
	☐	☐	☐	☐	☐	☐	☐

Seeds	Date Planted

Transplant	Date Planted

Seeds	Date Planted

Transplant	Date Planted

Monday

- [ ] _____
- [ ] _____
- [ ] _____
- [ ] _____

Tuesday

- [ ] _____
- [ ] _____
- [ ] _____
- [ ] _____

Wednesday

- [ ] _____
- [ ] _____
- [ ] _____
- [ ] _____

Thursday

- [ ] _____
- [ ] _____
- [ ] _____
- [ ] _____

Friday

- [ ] _____
- [ ] _____
- [ ] _____
- [ ] _____

Saturday

- [ ] _____
- [ ] _____
- [ ] _____
- [ ] _____

Sunday

- [ ] _____
- [ ] _____
- [ ] _____
- [ ] _____

Notes: _____

_____

_____

_____

Monday

_____

_____

_____

Tuesday

- ☐ _____
- ☐ _____
- ☐ _____
- ☐ _____

Wednesday

_____

_____

_____

Thursday

- ☐ _____
- ☐ _____
- ☐ _____
- ☐ _____

Friday

_____

_____

_____

Saturday

- ☐ _____
- ☐ _____
- ☐ _____
- ☐ _____

Sunday

- ☐ _____
- ☐ _____
- ☐ _____
- ☐ _____

Notes: _____

_____

_____

_____

Monday

- [ ] _____
- [ ] _____
- [ ] _____
- [ ] _____

Tuesday

- [ ] _____
- [ ] _____
- [ ] _____
- [ ] _____

Wednesday

- [ ] _____
- [ ] _____
- [ ] _____
- [ ] _____

Thursday

- [ ] _____
- [ ] _____
- [ ] _____
- [ ] _____

Friday

- [ ] _____
- [ ] _____
- [ ] _____
- [ ] _____

Saturday

- [ ] _____
- [ ] _____
- [ ] _____
- [ ] _____

Sunday

- [ ] _____
- [ ] _____
- [ ] _____
- [ ] _____

Notes: _____

_____

_____

_____

Monday

_____

_____

_____

Tuesday

☐ _____

☐ _____

☐ _____

☐ _____

Wednesday

_____

_____

_____

Thursday

☐ _____

☐ _____

☐ _____

☐ _____

Friday

_____

_____

_____

Saturday

☐ _____

☐ _____

☐ _____

☐ _____

Sunday

☐ _____

☐ _____

☐ _____

☐ _____

Notes: _____

_____

_____

_____

Stage Three: Maintenance

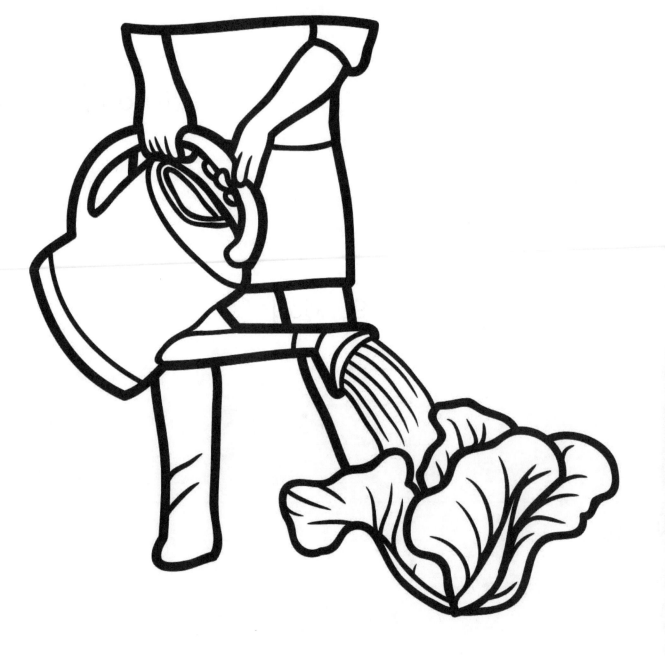

"What I need most of all are flowers, always, always."

– Claude Monet

1840-1926

TASK	M	T	W	T	F	S	S
	☐	☐	☐	☐	☐	☐	☐
	☐	☐	☐	☐	☐	☐	☐
	☐	☐	☐	☐	☐	☐	☐
	☐	☐	☐	☐	☐	☐	☐
	☐	☐	☐	☐	☐	☐	☐
	☐	☐	☐	☐	☐	☐	☐
	☐	☐	☐	☐	☐	☐	☐
	☐	☐	☐	☐	☐	☐	☐
	☐	☐	☐	☐	☐	☐	☐
	☐	☐	☐	☐	☐	☐	☐
	☐	☐	☐	☐	☐	☐	☐
	☐	☐	☐	☐	☐	☐	☐
	☐	☐	☐	☐	☐	☐	☐
	☐	☐	☐	☐	☐	☐	☐
	☐	☐	☐	☐	☐	☐	☐
	☐	☐	☐	☐	☐	☐	☐

TASK	M	T	W	T	F	S	S
	☐	☐	☐	☐	☐	☐	☐
	☐	☐	☐	☐	☐	☐	☐
	☐	☐	☐	☐	☐	☐	☐
	☐	☐	☐	☐	☐	☐	☐
	☐	☐	☐	☐	☐	☐	☐
	☐	☐	☐	☐	☐	☐	☐
	☐	☐	☐	☐	☐	☐	☐
	☐	☐	☐	☐	☐	☐	☐
	☐	☐	☐	☐	☐	☐	☐
	☐	☐	☐	☐	☐	☐	☐
	☐	☐	☐	☐	☐	☐	☐
	☐	☐	☐	☐	☐	☐	☐
	☐	☐	☐	☐	☐	☐	☐
	☐	☐	☐	☐	☐	☐	☐
	☐	☐	☐	☐	☐	☐	☐
	☐	☐	☐	☐	☐	☐	☐

TASK	M	T	W	T	F	S	S
	☐	☐	☐	☐	☐	☐	☐
	☐	☐	☐	☐	☐	☐	☐
	☐	☐	☐	☐	☐	☐	☐
	☐	☐	☐	☐	☐	☐	☐
	☐	☐	☐	☐	☐	☐	☐
	☐	☐	☐	☐	☐	☐	☐
	☐	☐	☐	☐	☐	☐	☐
	☐	☐	☐	☐	☐	☐	☐
	☐	☐	☐	☐	☐	☐	☐
	☐	☐	☐	☐	☐	☐	☐
	☐	☐	☐	☐	☐	☐	☐
	☐	☐	☐	☐	☐	☐	☐
	☐	☐	☐	☐	☐	☐	☐
	☐	☐	☐	☐	☐	☐	☐
	☐	☐	☐	☐	☐	☐	☐
	☐	☐	☐	☐	☐	☐	☐

TASK	M	T	W	T	F	S	S
	☐	☐	☐	☐	☐	☐	☐
	☐	☐	☐	☐	☐	☐	☐
	☐	☐	☐	☐	☐	☐	☐
	☐	☐	☐	☐	☐	☐	☐
	☐	☐	☐	☐	☐	☐	☐
	☐	☐	☐	☐	☐	☐	☐
	☐	☐	☐	☐	☐	☐	☐
	☐	☐	☐	☐	☐	☐	☐
	☐	☐	☐	☐	☐	☐	☐
	☐	☐	☐	☐	☐	☐	☐
	☐	☐	☐	☐	☐	☐	☐
	☐	☐	☐	☐	☐	☐	☐
	☐	☐	☐	☐	☐	☐	☐
	☐	☐	☐	☐	☐	☐	☐
	☐	☐	☐	☐	☐	☐	☐
	☐	☐	☐	☐	☐	☐	☐

Stage Four: Harvest

"In these golden October days no work is more fascinating than this getting ready for spring. The sun is no longer a burning enemy, but a friend, illuminating all the open space, and warming the mellow soil."

– Charles Dudley Warner
1829-1900

TASK	M	T	W	T	F	S	S
	☐	☐	☐	☐	☐	☐	☐
	☐	☐	☐	☐	☐	☐	☐
	☐	☐	☐	☐	☐	☐	☐
	☐	☐	☐	☐	☐	☐	☐
	☐	☐	☐	☐	☐	☐	☐
	☐	☐	☐	☐	☐	☐	☐
	☐	☐	☐	☐	☐	☐	☐
	☐	☐	☐	☐	☐	☐	☐
	☐	☐	☐	☐	☐	☐	☐
	☐	☐	☐	☐	☐	☐	☐
	☐	☐	☐	☐	☐	☐	☐
	☐	☐	☐	☐	☐	☐	☐
	☐	☐	☐	☐	☐	☐	☐
	☐	☐	☐	☐	☐	☐	☐
	☐	☐	☐	☐	☐	☐	☐
	☐	☐	☐	☐	☐	☐	☐

TASK	M	T	W	T	F	S	S
	☐	☐	☐	☐	☐	☐	☐
	☐	☐	☐	☐	☐	☐	☐
	☐	☐	☐	☐	☐	☐	☐
	☐	☐	☐	☐	☐	☐	☐
	☐	☐	☐	☐	☐	☐	☐
	☐	☐	☐	☐	☐	☐	☐
	☐	☐	☐	☐	☐	☐	☐
	☐	☐	☐	☐	☐	☐	☐
	☐	☐	☐	☐	☐	☐	☐
	☐	☐	☐	☐	☐	☐	☐
	☐	☐	☐	☐	☐	☐	☐
	☐	☐	☐	☐	☐	☐	☐
	☐	☐	☐	☐	☐	☐	☐
	☐	☐	☐	☐	☐	☐	☐
	☐	☐	☐	☐	☐	☐	☐
	☐	☐	☐	☐	☐	☐	☐